The Vale of Aylesbury In Camera

by Clive Birch FSA FRSA

QUOTES LIMITED of BUCKINGHAM

MCMXCI

Published by Quotes Limited
Buckingham, England

Typeset in Plantin by
Key Composition, Northampton, England

Pictures Lithographed by
South Midlands Lithoplates Limited, Luton, England

Printed by Busiprint Limited
Buckingham, England

Bound by Charles Letts Limited
Edinburgh, Scotland

© Clive Birch

ISBN 0 86023 401 0

One of the minor pleasures of the eighties has been the upsurge of interest in old postcards, instigating a flourishing trade, with fairs, dealers, auctions and even stands at jumble sales. For the inveterate collector of images of the past, this has been a boon, since many of these once prolific means of rapid communication have survived. People have kept messages from loved ones, pictures that once mattered to somebody somewhere, and the odd curiosity, so that more and more come onto the market. I am especially indebted to Julian Dunn for the way in which he has kept me supplied — some of these pictures passed through his hands.

As to family snaps, sepia scenes, glass plates and the occasional framed treasure, once again my friend of over 35 year, John Armistead, has copied other people's originals; I am ever in his debt. There are examples made available to me by Susan Cowdy, the Stanley H. Freese collection through James Venn, Ann Reed, Kay Fraser, and the W. M. Houston Collection, now deposited with the County, but originally lent to me by his son, Michael (possibly Kitchener 1920s photographs). This selection is only a small part of the pictures accumulated over the last decade. I am also indebted to Hugh Hanley, County Archivist and Julia Smith of the county's Historic Buildings Department for readily and effectively answering my queries.

Aylesbury Red Book for 1918
Beechwoods & Bayonets – Halton, Andrew E. Adam, Barracuda Books, 1983
The Book of Aylesbury, Clive Birch, Barracuda Books, 1976
Buckinghamshire Footpaths, J. H. B. Peel, Chaterson Ltd, 1949
The Bucks Advertiser Calendar & Guide to Aylesbury & District for 1911-12
Concise Oxford Dictionary of English Place Names, Eilert Ekwall, Oxford, (4th ed), 1960
Domesday Book: Buckinghamshire, ed John Morris, Phillimore, 1978
Echoes of old County Life, J. K. Fowler, Longman's, Green & Co, 1894
History and Antiquities of the County of Buckingham, George Lipscomb, J. & W. Robins, 1847
A History of Aylesbury, Robert Gibbs, 1885
History and Topography of Buckinghamshire, James Joseph Sheahan, Longman, 1862
A Life of John Hampden the Patriot 1594-1643, John Adair, MacDonald & Jane's, 1976
Maps of Bucks, Dr Gordon Wyatt, Barracuda Books, 1979
Post Office Directory of Northamptonshire, Huntingdonshire, Bedfordshire and Buckinghamshire, Kelly & Co, 1864 and 1887
Recollections of old Country Life, J. K. Fowler, Longman's, Green & Co, 1894
Records of Buckinghamshire, Bucks Archaeological Society, 1854 - date
Records of Old Times, J. Kersley Fowler ('Rusticus), Chatto & Windus, 1898
S. Mary's Church, Aylesbury, Parish Magazine, 1877 & 1878
Victoria History — Buckinghamshire, ed William Page, 1925 reprinted Dawsons of Pall Mall, 1969
Weedon Welcome, Kay Fraser, Sporting & Leisure Press, 1896

What exactly is the The Vale of Aylesbury? The 1974 administrative unit today embraces 350 square miles, 150,000 people and 109 parishes, including Aylesbury itself, Wendover, Winslow and Buckingham. But Wendover is hardly 'in' the Vale and Buckingham proudly regards itself as quite separate. Then again, the physical bounds have shifted — the Hertfordshire oakwood forests have long gone, and the myriad streams that diffused the plain and inhibited good husbandry have been drained, culverted, channeled or simply disappeared as population growth has lowered the water table.

In 1847 George Lipscomb had it thus: 'extending from the foot of the Chiltern Hills and the western border of Hertfordshire towards the north, to Wingrave and Oving, is skirted by the hills of Quainton and Pitchcott, and stretches westward almost to the verge of Oxfordshire'. Kelly's 1864 directory magisterially states it as 'large and fruitful' and 'long celebrated for verdure and fertility' — and then rather spoils the effect by lifting Lipscomb's words exactly without attributing them. Henry VIII's surveyor John Leland had the vale 'going one waye to the forest beyond Tame markett; it goeth otherwayes to Buckingham, to Stonye Stratford, to Newport Pagnell, and along from Aylesbury by the rootes of the Chilterne Hilles, almost to Dunstable', while William Camden gave it a passing nod — 'the whole Vale is commonly term'd the Vale of Ailsbury'. Robert Gibbs, in 1885, is a little more precise: 'The Chiltern Hills form the southern boundary . . . the Vale is watered by four brooks . . . which unite on the north-west and western verge of the parish . . .' but with typical caution, he adds 'The extent of the Vale of Aylesbury is not well defined'. Clare Read in 1856 limited it to Aylesbury, Hartwell, Stone, Winchendon, Waddesdon, Pitchcott, Dunton, Wing, Aston Abbots, Bierton and Broughton.

As to its appeal, Michael Drayton in his 1612 *Poly-Olbion* described it thus:

'For Alesbury's a vale that walloweth in her wealth
And (by her wholesome ayre continually in health)
Is lustie, firm and fat, and holds her youthfull strength.
Besides her fruitful earth, her mighty breadth and length,
Doth Chiltern fitly match: which mountainously hie,
And being very long, so likewise shee doth lie'.

It was certainly good farming country — and good huntin' country too, though 18th century commentator Arthur Young deplored the then lack of drainage, enclosure and crop rotation. He added: 'All this vale would make as fine meadows as any'. Within a century the Vale was fertile, efficiently farmed and prosperous, not to say booming. In 1862 James Sheahan described it as 'this large and beautiful crescent-shaped valley' and Camden said 'the Vale is almost all champain'.

It's all a matter of judgement and taste so, for the purposes of this book, the Vale is taken to include Aston Clinton, Halton and Weston Turville; the villages along the A413 as far as Winslow; the Claydons; Brill and its satellites despite their hills; the 'airport' country around Wing; and those places between Aylesbury, Thame and Bicester. Despite all, some are not represented through lack of suitable material, and Stewkley, Haddenham, Whitchurch and Long Crendon have been excluded because other books in this series cover them; Aylesbury is briefly represented, just to set the scene.

Thus, what follows is a selection, chosen for information, charm or historic significance, to supply facts about the past, and to entertain those who consider the Vale their home or their refuge — an affectionate portrait of a rich landscape, its places, and its people.

Aylesbury ducks in 1912 — fashion and farming practice diminished the roaring twenties trade; today turkeys are plumper and cheaper and frozen chicken breasts more cost-effective for consumer and packager alike. Aylesbury eats Brackley broiler and not the local pond product. In 1898 ducklings fetched 14s - £1 a couple, 'readily' in March/April, but they 'degenerate after leaving their native district'. Cottagers traditionally kept a 'set of ducks', selling the eggs to a 'ducker' who would raise some 5,000 head for eight or nine weeks before sale. Their fame rested on their pale flesh when plucked.

The Corn Exchange (later Town Hall) of 1865, County Hall and covered market, 1930s; the steps to County Hall were called the Gaol Stones in the early 19th century, when debtors exercised there. The statue to Lord Chesham, soldier of the Boer War, was unveiled on 14 July 1910. In 1918 Saturday was still market day, fat stock sales took place on Wednesday and there were several fairs throughout the year. In the 1950s the Market Square was still a meeting place — lunchtime saw a cross-section of county life strolling, stopping, speculating about the outcome of cases in the courthouse, and generally swapping stories. The development of Friars and destruction of the Market Square hinterland stopped all that. Today's Hale Leys and tomorrow's refurbished Friars may bring new life to the old heart of the town.

The War Memorial and Upper Market Square feature Hampden's statue, erected 27 July 1912 and moved in recent years; it faced a different way in the twenties. Hampden was the symbol of parliamentary freedom, and his London home was the site of today's 10 Downing Street. Reputedly killed by carbine shots to the shoulder, he may in fact have died from the discharge of an overprimed pistol and the loss of his hand. When his body was exhumed by Lord Nugent in 1830, the shoulder was unharmed, the hand missing. The symbolism of today's statue is now doubly significant. Tailors King & Sainsbury occupied the Round House, the Crown dominated the corner with High Street and Bradford's showrooms and warehouse presaged Kingsbury Square.

Church Street, St Mary's and the County Museum — currently undergoing major repairs; the Museum was opened in what was previously the headmaster's house and the Lower Endowed Schools. In 1912 'the collection of antiquities . . . is well arranged'. In 1854 George Gilbert Scott reported of St Mary's 'There has been a series of failures, repairs and re-failures from a very early to a very recent period'. Restoration commenced in 1855 and finished 14 years later. In 1974 the problem surfaced again, and again in 1984.

Edwardian High Street: John Wood at no 35 dispensed drugs and tested your sight, offering a darkroom for amateur photographers; A. T. Adkins of 112 & 120 repaired motor or cycle; 'all kinds of woodwork [were] made on the premises' by F. W. Horne at 27 while W. Roberts at 59 supplied Sanitary Bedding; the Aylesbury Co-operative Society (79-81) delivered machine-made bread daily; John Stephens ran The Fruit, Flower and Banana Stores at no 3 and the Waverley Temperance Hotel was opposite the Vale of Aylesbury Cycling and Athletic Club Ground. Ethel Smith at 51 sold underclothes, skirts, veilings, blouses, hosiery, gloves and 'millinery in all its branches'; Thomas Ward at 24 promised 'Pumps fitted on the most approved principle, and on Reasonable Terms', while F. Richings' Tea Rooms were at 31 & 33. You could get Fancy Boxes of Chocolates or Bronchial Tablets at H. Hopcraft's Confectionery Stores (no 71), William F. Morton cleaned windows from 106, and Messrs Gower & Adams ran the Crown tap at no 1, watched over by the Aylesbury Brewery Co at 5; Smith's Bank was at 19, next to the Congregational Church & Schools; the Post Office was at 26, St Joseph's iron Catholic Church at 64, J. Simmonds' Chandos Hotel four doors away, North & Randall's Mineral Water Factory at 82-84, the gasworks at 86, and LNWR station at 87, Stationmaster Mr R. Phizackerley.

The London and North Western railway station at the outbreak of war, 1914, welcomed a squadron of Lancers come to town on manoeuvres. Aylesbury was then served by the L & NW Railway to Euston, the Great Western to Paddington and the Great Central and Metropolitan from Baker Street and Marylebone — and there was a connection from Aylesbury to Cheddington. Today's single service is a pale echo of the days when Metroland mattered to the railwaymen.

A county town has many thirsts to slake. The King's Head has been satisfying travellers, farmers and residents for centuries. Here in 1910 two local labourers pause before taking ale; but temperance was in the ascendant in the 1870s when The Vale of Aylesbury Cocoa Houses Co Ltd was formed on the back of a successful British Workman's Public House, which had taken £214 7s 6d in 12 months. The new company would establish tea, coffee, cocoa and soup houses in town and Vale; £5000 worth of shares of 10s were offered. And in 1918 there was real choice: the Red Lion offered the 'Finest selection of Wines, Spirits & Cigars', Goodridge's Temperance Hotel had 'Hot Dinners, Teas &c Provided Daily', the George offered 'Suites . . . Billiard Rooms, extensive Stabling, Loose Boxes for Hunters, Good Accomodation for Motors', Mrs A. Horne supplied 'First-class commercial and cyclist accomodation . . . hot dinners daily 9d, 10d and 1s 3d . . . electrically lighted' at the Vale Hotel, the Greyhound provided 'Dinners, Luncheons, Teas, Chops, Steaks etc' and G. Gargini ran a 'specially appointed oyster room' at his Temple Street Fish Shop and at the Oyster Bar in the Bull's Head Hotel. In 1991 the Alcatraz was opened — an alcohol-free pub for over 15s. Nonetheless, where are you, Mrs Horne? Come back, Signor Gargini . . .

11

W. M. Keesey's charming sketch typifies the twenties and puts the Trust Houses' Bell Hotel on record — a victim of the mayhem that destroyed so much of the Market Square hinterland when Friars was built. It was here in the 19th century that the Volunteer Fire Brigade supped.

The Grammar School (built 1906) was a military hospital when this picture was taken. The school succeeded the 18th century Free School, itself preceded by the Latin School, first founded by Sir Henry Lee of Quarrendon, and then further endowed by Henry Phillips in 1714. On 21 February 1877 a public meeting discussed the future of the town's other, elementary schools, and decided they should remain voluntarily funded — although they were £300 in the red. School places were available for 1,453 by contrast to Government requirements for 1,166.

Hartwell House is now a hotel — and listed by Egon Ronay. For many years it hosted the County Show. The village finds its name from the 13th century Herdewelle or hart's spring. Sir Thomas Lee rebuilt the 17th century house in the mid-18th century. Louis XVIII came with his court to the house in 1808 and his queen died here of dropsy in 1810. When Louis was restored in 1814 he modelled a garden at Versailles on that of his wife at Hartwell. The eccentric Dr Lee lived here in the late 19th century, collecting Egyptian relics, improving the house, and opposing anything and everything from drink to religion. He also ran the Gooseberry Show, thus lending an early gastronomic note to today's restaurant for high-flyers. The winning berry brought its owner a copper tea-kettle, some of which must be sitting in local homes today, and elections brought great feasting to the house; the teetotallers 'made up by eating what they denied themselves of drinking'.

The Egyptian Springs at Hartwell recently restored, reflect one of Dr Lee's grand passions. He built up a collection of antiquities at Hartwell House, and created this tourist trap in 1856, architect Joseph Bononi — a Greek inscription declaims 'Water is best'.

Stone Church — the word 'stane' is old English from the 9th century — was built on a mound, possibly a barrow and heavily restored, mainly in 1843. It was consecrated on 1 June 1273. In 1852 the Bucks County Pauper Lunatic Asylum was built nearby for £43,500. The site was once a burial ground. Many of the psychiatric nurses who serve the county learnt their merciful trade here.

The County Arms at Stone was an ABC house. Early this century horse and trap were for hire — if you first went through to the bar. George Washington was the landlord in 1864 — he was also a gardener, as was his brother Samuel, who also retailed beer. Caring landlords left out a portable trough for the dray horse. Mrs Phillis Carter ran the Bugle Horn, a popular victualling house to this day.

The Avenue at Dinton — Dunn's or Dynne's 'tun' (homestead or village) — a place famed for John Bigg, recluse, who lived in a cave and patched his clothes rather than replace them, but less well known for the singular discoveries of 1859, when J. Y. Akerman claimed to have uncovered an Anglo-Saxon cemetery, with Romano-British pottery and a glass bottle of the time of Edward II: an extraordinary concatenation of antiquarian muddle.

Upper Green at Cuddington; Cudintuna in 1120, it was the tun of the people of Cuda, once famed for its medicinal springs and pillow lace. With the modern market moving to craft and cure-alls, there could be a future for Cuddington water and village frillies.

Church Street, Cuddington in 1906; the church was 'thoroughly restored' in 1858 by public subscription, and its foundation dates back beyond 1114. The Red Lion was run by Abraham Scott; George Scott ran the Fish. In addition, the village boasted the Seven Stars and White Swan.

In 1864 the Post Office at Cuddington did not exist — letters were mailed in a wall-box at 9 am and taken by foot messenger to Aylesbury, whence they were despatched at 'about 4 pm'. By the twenties Sidney Evans ran Post Office and stores; the White Barn is on the left. That was in the days when letters were delivered next day latest — and no nonsense about first, next day delivery or datapost either. And the sorting office wasn't at Milton Keynes . . .

The School at Ford, built in 1871 for 170 children, was run in the late 19th century by Clement E. Whitworth. What would he have made of the national curriculum?

The Bottle and Glass, an ABC house, at Littleworth, (more popularly know as Gibraltar), was also the postbox and bus stop, as well as selling Blue Bell tobacco in 1931. It was at Gibraltar (probably renamed from the gibbet, or gallows) that a carter from Thame was murdered; his assailant was hanged in 1823. The truck registration PP7775 would sell for a fortune today — and the carter's killer, if caught, would have walked free after time less remission for good behaviour.

The road through Dorton left a lot to be desired in 1904, when you consider that the name of the place means tun (or village) in a pass, from the old English 'duro' for door. There was a time when the chalybeate or iron spring gave forth 100 gallons a day, turning the grass black, such was its strength — the only comparable spring was in Germany. In the 1860s a pump room and baths were erected. But those were the days of outside privies and night soil, and baths were not for ordinary mortals.

Dorton House, built in the 17th century (1626) by Sir John Dormer Kt, was modernised in 1784 by Sir John Aubrey, and subsequently further restored, with some 20th century embellishments. It is now the private Ashfold School and has 'grown' numerous classrooms and a music room, recently created in an outbuilding.

The empties are out for collection at Lower (or Nether) Winchendon's Bear Inn in the '20s. The name is of uncertain origin, perhaps from 'wince', a roller or pulley, or even 'hleapewince', a lapwing.

The Post Office and village stores at Chearsley in 1940; Cerdeslai was 'Ceolred's leah' or meadow, where seven plough teams toiled in 1086.

Empire Day 1908 at Chearsley Hill saw the entire village in the uncertain sunshine — umbrellas well in evidence, and what must surely be a substantial intake of other places' children. Tradition holds that the lord's gallows stood here on the hill.

At Wood Siding, Brill Branch

METROPOLITAN and GREAT CENTRAL

Met Rly   GtC Rly

JOINT COMMITTEE

At Brill Station.

The Metropolitan and Great Central Railway produced these delicious postcards to publicise Metroland and beyond: here are Wood Siding, Brill Branch and Brill Station. 'Bre' was an old British name also found in Wales, meaning hill, and often reinforced with 'hyll', hence Bruhella or Brehull, now contracted to Brill.

In August 1935 the No 41 mixed train to Quainton Road leaves Brill Station, on the Brill Tramway. Once a polling place for MPs for the county, Brill in the 19th century boasted petty sessions at the Sun on alternate Fridays. With its annual fair at Michelmas, it prospered from brick and tile, as is evident from the lunar surface of its hill. Pottery was made there as far back as 1254 and until the late 1870s.

Brill Church, renovated in 1835, its bells recast ten years prior, had Norman columns and doors until some went in 1839 and '89 restorations. Kings stayed in Brill — Edward the Confessor had a hunting lodge here, and the Royal palace of the Plantagenets may have been near the Church. Brill was recorded a Royal borough in 1241 and again in 1316. Today it is a favourite of those bailiffs of our times, the estate agents; houses in Brill command a high price, even in a stagnant economy.

Muswell Hill at Brill, once a source of chalybeate mineral waters, is 744 ft above sea level and was also a trigonometrical survey station. Traces of Roman occupation were recorded here in 1908.

Oakley Road, Brill: Oakley was a charitable place. Saxon girl Aelfgeth held land here in return for teaching Sheriff Godric's daughter gold embroidery, and in the 1880s the poor's pasture extended to 115 acres, producing an annual £102, distributed to 34 poor people; another allotment bought greatcoats and calico and a third charity accumulated until it could afford apprenticeships for the sons of poor labourers.

Farm cart and road roller contrast old and new transport modes at the old cottages in Castle Street, Ludgershall in 1928. Tom Thomas reminded his Gran that he had sent a card once before 'the first time I went to camp' when 'the little bugler [was] leading the goat'. The scene was apparently unchanged for 'it only seems as yesterday'. He should see the infilling now. Lutegar gave his name to this 'gaershealh' or grazing ground, as Luttegersahala (1285) and John Wycliffe was the parish priest in 1368. This was Yates Stores.

West Hedge, Marsh Gibbon, the year after the Great War. Gibbon is a 12th century family name recorded in 1292 as Gibwyne, also reflected in Gubbins Hole Farm; Alric held it before and after Domesday, but he kept it at a price — 'harshly and wretchedly'. In the 1860s there were four pubs — Jacob's Well, White Hart, Greyhound and Plough, and one beer retailer. The Greyhound has kept its place and increased its reputation as an eating house.

Edgecote (after 'aecen', or oaks?) Church and House. Here there was a field called Gang Monday Land, which yielded an annual rent of £3 — distributed in cakes and ale: two of the former and as much of the latter as the tenants could drink. The balance, if any, went to the poor — a bit like the National Health.

Church and School, Grendon Underwood — the green hill under the wood, once recorded as Under Bernwode, the great forest that then stretched into north Bucks, and also once proclaimed as 'Grendon Underwood — The dirtiest town that ever stood'; roads were bad in winter at a time when the main route from Oxford ran through the village. Paradoxically, in summer, without wells and with the mile-distant spring run dry, the village was often without water. Shakespeare is said to have stayed here and Mr Skinner's 1882 Grendon Hall provides offices for Springhill Prison.

Challoners Hill, Steeple Claydon, with the school in the distance; the Claydon name stems from 'claeg' or 'claegig', clayey hill. Sir Thomas Chaloner, regicide, built a school in 1656 on the manorial waste; two hundred years later Lady Dunsany built another for girls and infants.

The famous Reading Room — latterly the almost closed Library, Steeple Claydon, gladly reprieved after much in-fighting — was an extended version of the schoolhouse built by Thomas Chaloner. Florence Nightingale contributed £50 to what was the first public library in an English village.

This 1930s shot shows a quieter village by the Camp Barn, and the thatched roofs for which the Claydons are renowned. The Camp was so named for Oliver's Camp — Cromwell's army camped there in early March 1644, leaving to besiege Hillesden House on the 3rd. Those weary warriors would hardly recognise the enlarged village of today, with its kerbside decor of parked cars, domesticated barns and the bijou boxes of the spec builders.

In Middle Claydon the children pose mid-road, when a gentler age saw horse and trap trundle by. A Saxon manor, it was bought by Sir Ralph Verney in 1465. The son of a later Ralph, Edmund the Royalist lost his life and left his hand at Edgehill in 1642. The estate passed into the Calverts by marriage; Sir Harry took the name Verney in 1827.

Middle Claydon almshouses in the twenties, moved here by the second Earl, originally stood near the churchyard, and were endowed by another Sir Ralph in the 1690s. Four flats provide the contemporary facility, where there were originally six homes.

Claydon House has not yet gained that slightly lost air, prevalent since the family retreated to their apartment, in what is now a National Trust set-piece treasure house, albeit beautifully maintained. The Giffards' Tudor mansion was rebuilt in the middle of the 18th century by Ralph, second Earl Verney. Mary, Baroness Fermanagh, pulled much of that down a century later, but kept the magnificent facade.

The thatched seat in Church Walk at Botolph Claydon; Botolph comes from 'botl', old English for building or, in this case, possibly manor, though Sheahan described it as a hamlet of East Claydon.

East Claydon — here in 1926 — was once a busy junction but by the 1860s the roads had disappeared due to the turnpike to Winslow. It embraced no less than three Norman manors, and its 13th century church was severely damaged in the Civil War and virtually rebuilt in the 1820s.

Westcott House (clearly marked on the reverse as 'Joseph's home') was on land largely owned by the Dukes of Buckingham and Marlborough in 1860. That included Philosophy Farm, which dates from the 1618 will of Sir William Sedley; he left £200 to endow a lecture in Natural Philosophy at Oxford; the lands first bought were exchanged in 1774 for the farm.

Another of those delightful Metroland cards this time shows Verney Junction — where you could catch the train to Brackley and Oxford — and Quainton Mill, which a Mr Foster promised to swallow 'if they would give him time', along with 6lbs of bacon, a peck of potatoes, a quartern loaf and a gallon of ale, all consumed in three hours.

Waddesdon Manor station on the Metropolitan & Great Central Joint Railway; chocolate and stamp machines jostle house sale posters, milk churns await collection, there's a parcel service, and wicker cages contain local duck in this Edwardian study of the Rothschild era.

This is High Street, Waddesdon early this century, when children could play in the road with impunity, smocked and straw hatted, and a baby had a home-made pushchair. In 1862 an alms cow was kept at Lodge Hill — the milk went to the 'aged poor'. Before 1825 there were two such cows. Now there are none. The Five Arrows (on the left) was rebuilt by Baron Rothschild, landlord Henry Turner.

Waddesdon Reading Room was provided in 1883 by Baron Ferdinand de Rothschild, who built the village hall in 1897 and rebuilt Arthur Godwin's 17th century almshouses in 1894. Such paternalism is unfashionable today, though it gave benefit in short order to small places like this before there were planners to draft structure plans, and structure plans to stop what locals want, while seeking bland infill for urban incomers.

The Rothschild mansion — Waddesdon Manor — with a marquee in the garden, as if there was insufficient room in the house itself. Baron Lionel bought the land for £55,000, spent £87,000 on the house and another £1,858,000 fitting it out. Unlike Mentmore, where the current Enlightenment reflects a new richesse, the National Trust looks after this house.

Weohtgar, later Wott or Wett, gave his name to his 'dun' or hill, home to nearly 200 souls in Norman times. And the Rothschilds gave the Manor this splendid rockery — a self-contained vista in a 'garden room' of which even David Stephens would be proud.

The ruins at Quarrendon (Cweorndun, or 'hill where millstones were got') are where Sts Osyth and Edith were said to be born. Osyth's aunt, St Edith, is believed to have founded a 'monasterium' in Aylesbury. In the mid-19th century controversy raged over this building, probably a 1294 chapel, (possibly even earlier), flood-damaged in the 16th century but still in use in 1746; it was falling apart by 1817. In the latter part of the last century it was cannibalised for timber by farmers, stone by labourers — one farmer built a garden house from it — and marble by an Aylesbury candlestick maker. In 1592 Sir Henry Lee gave the 'Masque at Quarendon' for good Queen Bess — 'with great splendor and magnificence'.

The Five Elms, Weedon — another ABC house-in the '20s: Ezra Welch, bricklayer, was landlord in 1864; before him, three Thorns had filled the post for exactly one hundred years — Elizabeth, Provis and Richard. By 1887, Alfred Honour was in charge, followed by Lacey, Jones, Brandon, Bonniface, Sewell, Hart, Hedge, Macguire (a few months only), Thatcher and Rixon. In the '60s the Frasers arrived and revived the customs of hunt stirrup cups and the Weedon feast, last held in 1913 — music, dance, pies and ale. They even brought back the 17th century ale conner or taster.

Children gather outside the village stores at Weedon. At the turn of the century, when this picture was taken, they went to Dr Bridle's school at Hardwick, built in 1871. Mrs Martha Roberts was the mistress in charge of 12 girls; the original 18 boys had become 45 when David Roberts was Master.

The younger generation has clearly followed the cameraman from the stores to the 1892 Primitive Methodist chapel at Weedon in this early 20th century shot. The original Wesleyan Chapel was put up in 1854. Weodun was a temple hill when the Saxons were here. The village included 27 acres of Poors Allotments given by Lady Nugent in 1848.

Hardwick (or 'heordl(e) wic', a 'wic' or farm for the flock of sheep): the Church, renowned for its monuments, includes one in the churchyard to 247 slain in the 1643 battle of Aylesbury. In 1873 the Church was restored at a cost of £4,000 by G. E. Street.

Hardwick Rectory was where a stableyard door bore a carved date of 1551. Sheahan called it a 'genteel and commodious residence'. Here Rev Christopher Erle often hosted the meet and followed Baron Rothschild's hounds 'to promote Christianity amongst the Jews'. A 'famous breakfast' was laid out, with a fine ham which Rev Erle assured the Baron was 'a mutton ham' and once, when the Duke of Grammont fell in a ditch, Erle tried to persuade the Baron to help him out, so he could baptise him.

Ducks gambol in the ford at Hardwick — an idyll invaded by the new telegraph. It was no idyll 900 years ago, when the population was 100 — plus eight slaves.

Grandborough ('grenebeorge' or green hill) Church in 1921 — it suffered in the Civil War at the hands of Cornelius Holland. He was a Royal kitchen scullion who prospered in the King's service, betrayed him, and destroyed the chancels of several churches, including this one in the village of his birth. It dates to the early 14th century and was restored by Sir Gilbert Scott in 1881. Vicar Stubbs started a Co-op with £8-9, not enough for a cow, so a workman said 'spell it with an S' and they bought two sows. In four months they had 18 piglets — that's co-operation.

The commercial centre of North Marston (or tun by a marsh) in 1905 — with the Bell Inn. Bootmaker James Garner was the landlord in 1887; 25 years earlier it was James Holden. The other pubs were the Wheatsheaf and Armed Yeoman.

North Marston Church belonged to the Abbey of Eynsham, then Dunstable Priory. 1290-1314 Rector John Schorne was so pious his knees 'became horny by the frequency of his prayers'; he was credited with miracles — the waters from the village well were believed to heal — and the man himself was alleged to have imprisoned 'the evil one' in one of his boots, for which he was not canonised, as legend insists. The well spring never failed, and the waters never froze, but in 1835 it was brought into general use for drinking water. The village promptly suffered a fever, but thereafter escaped all sickness.

In this Great War study of Swanbourne, taken in an obviously hot August, Nell wrote 'No Tommies here, so I don't wear my hat!' Happily, the village's name calls up the identical image from which it is taken — the stream of swans. It was not so lucky in the Civil War, when the King's forces 'have this day fired a country village, called Swanburne, . . . because they were not willing to be plundered of all they had'. That was 16 May 1643.

Swanbourne House, now a school, was bought by the Fremantles at the end of the 18th century. Vice Adml Sir Thomas F. Fremantle distinguished himself at Copenhagen and Trafalgar. The naval tradition lives on, with the present Lord Lieutenant, the Hon Cdr John Fremantle of Swanbourne. Appropriately enough, it was Lady Fremantle who established a straw plait school but it had gone by the 1880s, when the then Fremantle, Lord Cottesloe, supported the 1871 infants' school.

LEFT: An unusual Harvest Festival picture in Mursley Church; as long ago as 1230 Mursley had a weekly market, and another from 1243, because it was en route from Buckingham to Dunstable, and a good deal larger than Winslow. Aylesbury's rise and Buckingham's decline reduced its importance. At one time Bucks farmers held their own harvest-home festival, hosting local tradesmen and farmworkers, perhaps forty in all, with 'a round of beef, and a haunch of mutton with the goodly addition of plumpudding, . . . plenty of good beer . . . pipes and tobacco', an address by the host, songs and jokes, 'until near midnight'. 'It would have been against the spirit and public opinion of the time to have sent one's guests home sober.' RIGHT: Mursley Grange; was there ever someone called Myrsa? Noone knows. If there was, this was his meadow or clearing.

The postman has just collected from the post office stores at Mursley in this 1913 shot by photographer Turnham. Only 20 years before, there was no post office as such: Ann Bowler received letters for the once daily service via Winslow.

E. Cleaver, of Wing post office, published this early 20th century picture of Park Road. In 966 it was Weowungum — Weohthun's people and over 100 lived here in 1086. In 1527 the Church was rich in gold, silver and gilt; it had ten chalices and a silver censer, plus 20 books, and satin, lawn and velvet cloths for the altar. Where have they all gone? Road, railway and canal lent it significance, but the '60s threat of a third London airport brought it national prominence, when the natives rebelled — and won in 1971. Once a market town, chartered in 1255, it looked more to Leighton Buzzard than Aylesbury, with a daily carrier at the end of the last century. Today it straddles the main road between the two, to its detriment.

Amateur night at Aston Abbots — where the photographer crudely wrote on the front of his picture 'The abby lodge and drive'. The name reflects the eastern (holding of the) abbey or abbots of St Albans, who held it from Norman times.

Troops water their horses at Wingrave (the grove of Wing) in the build-up to the Great War, 1914. Villagers line the rails with some apprehension, though the lads on the left seem unconcerned — a peaceful harbinger of a time of sacrifice. As American B52s thunder across our skies in 1991, it might serve as a timely reminder of the risks others run for our way of life.

C. L. Pond of the General Stores on The Green published this postcard of the High Street looking south at Cheddington in 1927. Cetta's dun or hill might perhaps have been a hut on the hill — from 'cete', old English for hut, but when the Normans came, Fin the Dane was in charge — and he kept his lands.

When Cheddington Church was restored, remnants of a Norman structure were found. The 1858 works were funded in part by a mortgage on the church rates — an unusual arrangement. Earl Brownlow and rector Arthur Perceval Purêy-Cust paid the rest, in the days when aristocrats and priests had the means so to do.

Marsworth Church; the village lay on the Icknield Way, the L & NW Railway line, and the Grand Junction Canal. The church was restored in 1828, 1854, 1860, 1868 and again in the late 1880s, when strawplait dealer William Boddington typified the old order and Thomas Mead the new with his steampowered mill, while Daniel Hudman and William Thomas reflected the importance of the canal as toll collector and overseer respectively.

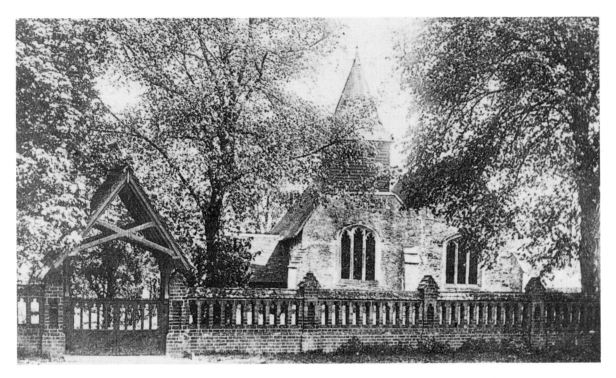

Hulcott Church — the settlement was Hucca's cot — is believed to date beyond its more obvious 1330 origins. Certainly the rectors can be traced to 1270. The building was restored in 1863, and the work started the year before, when the Church of England School was established for 27 children, Miss Newham the mistress in charge.

Bierton was the tun by the burg (of Aylesbury). Here is the Church, a 14th century structure re-roofed in 1636, formed from a chapelry of Aylesbury in 1266. Fifteen acres of allotments were endowed in 1786, and in the 1860s 'a score or so of elderly women continue to make lace, both black and white' and 'a portion of the inhabitants plait straw'. A field in the parish was called Corbet's Piece, after a ratcatcher and chimney sweep from Tring, who climbed down Richard Holt's chimney and murdered him in his bed on 7 June 1773. He was hanged and gibbeted in the corner of the field. In 1795 the skull still hung in the gibbet chains; the gibbet post lasted as a gatepost until 1860, when it was carved into 'fancy articles'. Where are they now?

This two-wheeled timber bob was being loaded between St Leonard's and Aston Hill at Aston Clinton in 1935 when Stanley Freese took this shot. 3,000 years ago a Bronze Age warrior dropped his knife dagger here. In the late 19th century, the 'township' was dominated by 16 straw plait dealers out of 74 commercial interests. Sadly the willow-chip maker had gone, but the ropemaker was still in business.

The Swan and the Institute at Aston Clinton; other pubs included the Oak, Half Moon & Seven Stars, White Lion, Plumber's Arms, Waggon & Horses, Stag's Head, New Bell, and Bull's Arms — in 1864 — joined within 25 years by the Rose & Crown, Partridge's Arms, and Rothschild's Arms, possibly a renaming of one that had by then vanished off the lists. One that has not vanished is the Bell, one of the more consistent performers in post-war haute cuisine, country-style.

'Would you like a duck for dinner?' Lily asked Bessie Prior when she sent this picture of Aylesbury ducks at Weston Turville in 1909. The placename comes from Tureuill, the 12th century landholder. Food was also on Widow Turpin's mind in 1736 when she left money for 'groat(sic) loaves of good and Wholesome bread' for 'the poorest inhabitants', not surprisingly in need, for as late as 1908 straw plait was still being made.

W. H. Christmas of Aylesbury Road, Wendover was the camp photographer at Halton: 'Here is another plane, the Andover ambulance. It has a 650hp RR Condor engine and carries 8 passengers. The man on the top is a flight sergeant and is probably about to start the engine. Notice that in a heavy bus like this the tail is supported on a little carriage to prevent the tail skids being damaged. See also the long exhaust pipe which makes sure no fumes enter the cabin.' RAF Halton was a product of Alfred Rothschild's patriotism; timber for the Kaiser's war, then the estate itself went to the Army, and finally the airmen. His grand house, now the Officers' Mess, succeeded what was described in 1847 as the Mansion House 'a plain, unostentatious building' with 'a fine view over the Vale . . . Bosom'd high in tufted trees'.

On the edge of the Vale, the Chilterns rise up to the Burnham plateau. On this farewell scene — 'Buckinghamshire in Winter' — there is a short verse: 'You be Jack, and I'll be Jill, Full of fun and laughter, I'll toboggan down the hill, You come tumbling after' — into the Vale of Aylesbury . . .

Index to Illustrations